RING AROUND THE ROSIE

Retold by STEVEN ANDERSON

Illustrated by GINA PERRY

CANTATA LEARNING

WWW.CANTATALEARNING.COM

CANTATA
LEARNING

Published by Cantata Learning
1710 Roe Crest Drive
North Mankato, MN 56003
www.cantatalearning.com

Library of Congress Control Number: 2015932816
Anderson, Steven
Ring Around the Rosie / retold by Steven Anderson; Illustrated by Gina Perry
Series: Tangled Tunes
Audience: Ages: 3–8; Grades: PreK–3
Summary: In this twist on the classic song "Ring Around the Rosie," jump up and down and all around as you sing along.
ISBN: 978-1-63290-361-7 (library binding/CD)
ISBN: 978-1-63290-492-8 (paperback/CD)
ISBN: 978-1-63290-522-2 (paperback)
1. Stories in rhyme. 2. Weather—fiction. 3. Games—fiction.

Book design and art direction, Tim Palin Creative
Editorial direction, Flat Sole Studio
Music direction, Elizabeth Draper
Music arranged and produced by Drew Temperante

Printed in the United States of America in North Mankato, Minnesota.
122015 0326CGS16

Have you ever played Ring Around the Rosie? Did you know that children around the world have been playing this game for years? In England, children call it Ring a Ring o' Roses.

Now turn the page, and then join hands with your friends as you sing along!

Ring around the rosie,
a pocket full of **posies**,
ashes, ashes,
we all fall down!

Sitting in the **meadow**,
looking at a rainbow,
thunder, **lightning**,
we all jump up!

Ring around the rosie,
a pocket full of posies,
ashes, ashes,
we all fall down!

Lying on the green grass,
watching all the clouds pass,
thunder, lightning,
we all jump up!

Ring around the rosie,
a pocket full of posies,
ashes, ashes,
we all fall down!

Waiting in the backyard,
hoping to see the stars,
thunder, lightning,
we all jump up!

Ring around the rosie,
a pocket full of posies,
ashes, ashes,
we all fall down!

SONG LYRICS

Ring Around the Rosie

Ring around the rosie,
a pocket full of posies,
ashes, ashes,
we all fall down!

Sitting in the meadow,
looking at a rainbow,
thunder, lightning,
we all jump up!

Ring around the rosie,
a pocket full of posies,
ashes, ashes,
we all fall down!

Lying on the green grass,
watching all the clouds pass,
thunder, lightning,
we all jump up!

Ring around the rosie,
a pocket full of posies,
ashes, ashes,
we all fall down!

Waiting in the backyard,
hoping to see the stars,
thunder, lightning,
we all jump up!

Ring around the rosie,
a pocket full of posies,
ashes, ashes,
we all fall down!